How Benjamin Franklin Became a Revolutionary in Seven (Not-So-Easy) Steps

How **Benjamin**

Franklin
Became a
Revolutionary
in Seven (Not-So-Easy) Steps

Gretchen Woelfle   Illustrated by John O'Brien

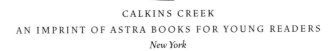

CALKINS CREEK

AN IMPRINT OF ASTRA BOOKS FOR YOUNG READERS

New York

To Blue Jay, Lilah, and Silas
and
Ayala, Harel, and Nadav
—GW

For Joanne and Hannah —JO

Benjamin Franklin was a proud citizen of America all his life.

And a proud subject of the British Empire.

Until he wasn't.

It took nearly seventy years and seven not-so-easy steps to turn Benjamin Franklin from a loyal British subject to a British traitor—and a fired-up American revolutionary.

Here's how it happened.

"Being ignorant is not so much a Shame, as being unwilling to learn."

'Twas a special day!

Seven-year-old Benjamin Franklin had a pocket full of pennies, so he strolled down the streets of Boston to the toy store. On his way, he met a boy playing a shiny tin whistle.

He stopped to listen. The boy played on.

Benjamin loved that shiny whistle!

He wanted that whistle!

He wanted that whistle so much he emptied his pocket and gave the boy all his pennies—every single one.

Benjamin wasn't shy about getting what he wanted.

Home he went, tooting his whistle all the way. He tooted in the kitchen . . . in the bedrooms . . . in the workshop where his father stirred smelly vats of soap . . . in the shop where his mother sold the soap, made from a secret family recipe . . .

"STOP!" cried his mother and father and brothers and sisters and cousins.

Benjamin stopped long enough to tell them how he spent all his pennies for his wonderful whistle. Everyone laughed.

"You paid *four times* more than it was worth," they told him.

They kept on laughing, but Benjamin cried with vexation. His shiny whistle wasn't fun anymore.

STEP #1

Benjamin Franklin learned early, "Do not give too much for the Whistle."

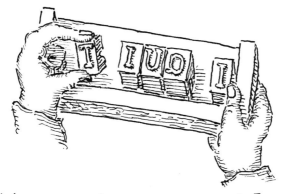

"Anger is never without a Reason, but seldom with a good One."

After just two years of school, twelve-year-old Benjamin Franklin went looking for a trade. He and his father roamed the town, stopping here to visit a blacksmith, there a cutler, and down the lane a carpenter. Benjamin marveled at the tradesmen's skills, but he couldn't see himself working in those shops.

They dropped in on his older brother James, a printer and newspaper publisher.

Now that caught Benjamin's fancy! He loved words. He was a voracious reader.

So he signed on as James's apprentice. Benjamin promised to work for him for nine years and learn all about printing and publishing.

During the day, he set frames of lead type and ran the

printing press. He was a fast learner, a hard worker, and a strong lad. He could carry two trays of heavy lead type up a flight of stairs, while the other apprentices could barely manage one.

At night, Benjamin borrowed books from a friend who worked for a bookseller. He read poetry and books about politics, science, religion. He was curious about *everything*! He was careful not to smudge the pages and returned the books in the morning before the bookshop opened. When he had a bit of money, he bought books of his own.

Benjamin read the latest news in James's newspaper,

The New-England Courant. He also read witty letters written by clever young men who hung around the print shop. He thought himself as clever as they were. He'd try his hand at writing.

Meanwhile bold brother James had dared to criticize Massachusetts politicians in his paper and was thrown in jail for a few weeks.

Bold Benjamin wrote letters to the *Courant*, signing them "Mrs. Silence Dogood." He disguised his handwriting and slipped the letters under the front door.

Mrs. Dogood, a sassy widow, railed against women's ridiculous hoop skirts, "blockhead" college boys, religious hypocrites, and town drunkards. "She" spoke up for educating women and defending "the rights and liberties of my country." Any attempt to take them away was sure "to make my blood boil exceedingly."

Benjamin spiced Silence Dogood's complaints with humor and stayed out of jail. He wrote fourteen Dogood letters for the *Courant* and readers loved them. But when

James discovered that his sixteen-year-old brother had duped him, *his* blood boiled exceedingly!

As for Benjamin, he hated taking orders from James.

Two stubborn brothers—it was bound to end badly.

And it did.

Benjamin had only worked five years of his nine-year contract, but that was enough for him!

He sold his books to buy his passage on a ship. Then he stole onboard after dark, and left James in the lurch.

STEP #2

Benjamin Franklin rebelled when he thought his "rights and liberties" were violated.

"Diligence
is the Mother of Good-Luck."

Benjamin Franklin, seventeen, landed in Philadelphia in 1723 with just a few coins in his pocket, no friends, and no job.

A mighty challenge for an enterprising lad!

He was ready for it.

He found work with a slipshod printer and soon proved himself better than his boss. He made friends with all sorts of people—poor apprentices, rich merchants, and even the royal governor. Seven years later, he opened his own print shop.

Franklin meant to become the best *and* the hardest working *and* the richest printer in Philadelphia.

He made sure his neighbors saw him working late at night and early in the morning.

He made sure they saw that he was not too proud to push a wheelbarrow full of paper through the streets.

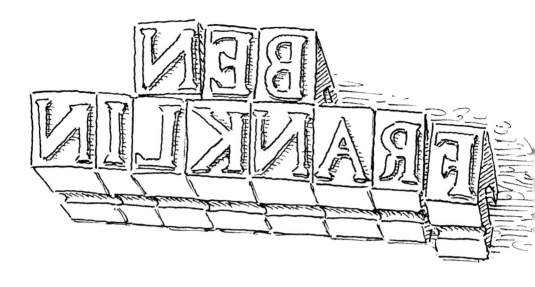

And that's not all.

To make sure he got the top-quality paper he wanted, he invested in several paper mills. Then he went a step further and started selling that paper to other printers. He became the largest paper supplier in the colony.

And that's not all.

Franklin hired printers' apprentices. He opened a shop and sold books, magazines, groceries, and his Boston family's homemade soap.

He published a newspaper, *The Pennsylvania Gazette,* which became the most respected newspaper in Philadelphia.

Franklin informed his readers about local news, news from other colonies, and news from Britain. He also entertained them by printing letters that poked fun at leaders as well as ordinary folks. Silence Dogood remained silent, but Franklin (and other secret authors) signed their letters Martha Careful, Caelia Shortface, Alice Addertongue, Harry Meanwell, and Anthony Afterwit.

And that's not all.

He became the official printer of Pennsylvania and New Jersey. He designed and printed paper money—and made the designs so complicated that counterfeiters couldn't copy them. He was shrewd as well as skillful.

And on top of all that . . .

Every year, he wrote and published *Poor Richard's Almanack*, a runaway best seller filled with farming advice, weather predictions, and recipes. Dozens of such almanacs

were published each year in the colonies. But Franklin's included something special: the life and times of a hapless character named Richard Saunders and his wife, Bridget, who scolded him for being so poor.

"Poor Richard"—Franklin in disguise—filled the *Almanack* with funny stories and clever sayings that we still remember today. It sold in all thirteen colonies and made Franklin a household name. People from New England to Georgia began to talk about that inventive printer from Philadelphia.

STEP #3

Benjamin Franklin mastered the power of pen and press to inform, persuade, and entertain the public.

Poor Richard Says . . .

'Tis easier to prevent bad habits than to break them.

The doors of wisdom are never shut.

What you
would seem to be,
be really.

A true Friend is the best possession.

He that waits upon fortune is never sure
of a dinner.

People who are wrapped up
in themselves make small
packages.

Years later, Benjamin admitted that in his apprentice days, he "perhaps [had been] too saucy and provoking" to his brother James. The two reconciled before James died at age thirty-eight, and Benjamin took on James's son, Jemmy, as an apprentice. When Jemmy completed his contract, Franklin offered to set him up in his own printing business. Jemmy refused. Instead, he went home to help his widowed mother run the family newspaper. The young man proved to be as bold and independent as his father and his uncle!

"The Good particular Men may do separately . . . is small, compared with what they may do collectively."

Every Friday night Benjamin Franklin and eleven other young tradesmen got together for a meeting of the Junto, begun in 1727 and named after a London men's club. This was Franklin's brainchild—a social club, a professional network, and an educational forum. Four printers, a shoemaker, a silversmith, a carpenter, a glazier, a surveyor, and a few clerks began the meetings by filling their glasses with wine and exchanging the week's gossip:

Which businesses are prospering or failing? Does your business need help from the Junto? Has someone damaged your good name? Can we help you to right this wrong?

Then on to the main event of the evening.

Like Franklin, few of the Junto members had much formal schooling, but they all possessed "the sincere Spirit of Enquiry after Truth." Their interests ranged far beyond printing and shoemaking to include politics, mathematics, science, astronomy, poetry, and philosophy. Every week, one member tackled a thorny issue and presented his thoughts to the club:

Can a poor man become rich and still remain an honest man?

If a government deprives citizens of their rights, should they resist?

How can the laws in our colony be improved?

When the lecture was over, talk flowed as freely as the wine. The men questioned, agreed, and argued with each other, all with good cheer.

The Junto members, booklovers like Franklin, borrowed each other's books. But they wanted more to choose from. So Franklin proposed they start a library, open to the public for a small fee. With the fees they bought more books and rented a room to store them. And so the Library Company of Philadelphia was born. It's still around today, with some of the Junto's original books on its shelves.

Benjamin Franklin had more bright ideas to spruce up his city, but he didn't work alone. He convinced others—friends, neighbors, strangers—to work with him.

No one liked stumbling through the muddy Philadelphia streets after dark so Franklin started a campaign to pave the streets and light them at night.

Wooden houses with open fireplaces often went up in flames. We'll organize a fire brigade, Franklin said, to prevent fires from spreading. With Franklin in the lead, they did. (A few years later, he came up with an invention to prevent some of those fires from starting in the first place.)

It's time that a fine city like Philadelphia had a college, Franklin said. He assembled a group of leading citizens and the College of Philadelphia rose up. Later, it became the University of Pennsylvania.

Philadelphia had no hospital. Franklin thought up a new way to raise money—a matching fund. He got the Pennsylvania Assembly to give half the money if citizens donated the other half. It worked! A few people grumbled that Franklin had been too devious. He knew he was not devious, but ingenious. And Philadelphia got its hospital.

When people wanted something done, they called on Benjamin Franklin—the most popular man in Philadelphia. And he called on his friends and neighbors.

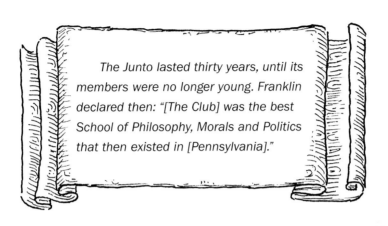

The Junto lasted thirty years, until its members were no longer young. Franklin declared then: "[The Club] was the best School of Philosophy, Morals and Politics that then existed in [Pennsylvania]."

STEP #4

Benjamin Franklin saw that a good leader needed a good team behind him.

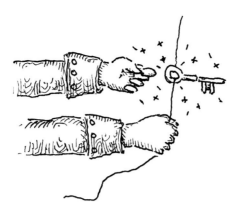

"Hide not your Talents, they for Use were made. What's a Sun-Dial in the Shade!"

When Benjamin Franklin turned forty-two in 1748, he had saved enough money to retire from printing. But he didn't retire from learning, exploring, and inventing.

Franklin had seen parlor tricks using electrical shocks and sparks and couldn't resist inventing a few of his own. He amused friends when he sent his electrically charged mechanical spider skittering across a table.

He hung a portrait of King George on his wall and urged visitors to touch the royal crown—which gave them a (small) shock. Was this a lesson for Americans: that kings can be dangerous?

No. Franklin was a loyal British subject. It was just a parlor trick.

Franklin loved practical jokes, but he was dead serious about his new project—electricity. "I never was before engaged in any study that so totally engrossed my attention," he later wrote.

He read all the electrical research reports from Europe. No one had figured out just what electricity was or how it worked. And no one had found a practical use for it.

Franklin was about to change that!

He ordered glass tubes and jars from England. He ransacked his kitchen for thimbles, a vinegar cruet, a cake of wax, and a pump handle. He turned his home library into a laboratory and gathered a team to help. They included three Junto members: a silversmith to make lab equipment, a mathematician, and a lawyer.

For the next three years, Franklin performed dozens of experiments in his lab. Some of them came to nothing, but others led him to unlock some of the secrets of electricity.

He found a way to store electricity and created an early battery.

He proved that an electrical current was a single "fluid" with positive and negative charges, not two "fluids" like others had thought.

Ever the wordsmith, Franklin created a new electrical vocabulary: *positive* and *negative charge, plus* and *minus, battery.* He apologized for these words, saying that others would probably find better ones to describe how electricity worked.

No one has. We still use his words today. In fact, one
measurement of electrical current is called a "franklin."

Venturing outdoors, Franklin tested his theory that
lightning bolts contain huge charges of electricity. He built
a kite with a pointed wire on top and tied a metal key to the

bottom of the kite string. During a thunderstorm, he touched his knuckle to the key and got a shock.

He was lucky not to be killed!

Franklin, still alive, had proved that electricity occurs in huge amounts in nature. In fact, it is a major physical force like gravity, heat, light, and magnetism.

Franklin, being Franklin, wanted to find a helpful use for electricity.

He had proved that lightning was electrical.

He had seen metal swiftly conducting an electrical current.

He had also seen lightning strikes burn down houses.

What if he attached a long, iron rod reaching above the rooftop, down the side of a building, into the ground?

That rod should draw lightning away from buildings and prevent them from bursting into flame.

It did indeed.

Franklin printed instructions for building a lightning rod in *Poor Richard's Almanack*, and, before long, he saw his invention sprouting on rooftops all over Philadelphia.

When he sent reports of his work to England and France, the reports caused shock waves among scientists. Franklin had solved problems that had baffled electrical researchers for fifty years. His work took electricity from the realm of parlor tricks to the halls of science.

He was elected to the top scientific societies in Europe. Five universities in England, Scotland, and America gave him honorary degrees and a new title: Dr. Franklin. He became the most famous American in Europe.

Not bad for a lad with just two years of schooling!

STEP #5

Benjamin Franklin's celebrity status served him well in years to come.

"History is full of the Errors of States and Princes."

Success as a printer, publisher, author, community leader, scientist, and inventor would have been enough for most men. Not Benjamin Franklin.

He had even bigger dreams.

America was growing fast. The population was exploding. Immigrants were coming from countries other than Great Britain. And white men could vote for town councils and colonial assemblies to pass laws to govern themselves. American colonial governments were modeled on the Parliament of Great Britain. Franklin, and many others, were thriving in the British American colonies.

Slavery, legal in all thirteen colonies in the mid-1700s, was a monstrous blot on the bright picture of American life. Few white people questioned slavery in Franklin's lifetime. For a time, he himself owned several enslaved servants and advertised slave sales in his newspaper. But he came to see that slavery was morally wrong, and "the whites who have slaves, not laboring, are enfeebled."

Franklin supported schools for Black children and saw that they were just as capable as white children. He humbly confessed, "You will wonder perhaps that I should ever doubt it, and I will not undertake to justify all my Prejudices." In 1787, Franklin became president of the Pennsylvania Society for Promoting the Abolition of Slavery. In February of 1790, just weeks before he died, he presented a petition for abolition to Congress. They rejected it.

Franklin, a leader in Philadelphia, dreamed of becoming a leader in Pennsylvania . . . and maybe in all British America. He ran for the Pennsylvania Assembly in 1751 and won. Being a lawmaker, he believed, "would enlarge my Power of doing Good." But he confessed that it also fed his ambition.

Franklin dove into Pennsylvania politics with gusto. He soon took a leading role in keeping the peace between English settlers and Indians, both threatened by the French.

French soldiers and renegades had been attacking inland British settlements from New York to Virginia. The French didn't bother the British settlements along the Atlantic coast. But they plotted to control the lands along the Ohio River and west of the Appalachian Mountains from Canada to Louisiana.

In 1754, Franklin and three other Pennsylvanians sailed up the Hudson River to Albany, New York, on a peace mission. They joined twenty delegates from six other colonies to negotiate with the Haudenosaunee, a powerful group of six Indian nations. The colonies needed their help to repel French attacks.

But Franklin saw another problem—not the French, not the Indians, but the colonies themselves. When one colony suffered a French attack and asked for help, the neighboring colonies shrugged their shoulders and said, not our problem.

Franklin saw a solution. He took to heart the words of Canasatego, the Haudenosaunee leader (translated from his own language): "Our wise Forefathers established Union and Amity [friendship] between the [Six] Nations; this has made us formidable. . . . We are a powerful Confederacy, and by your observing the same Methods our wise Forefathers have taken, you will acquire fresh Strength and Power."

Union and friendship for fresh strength and power.

This was Franklin's way of doing things!

After promises were made between the Haudenosaunee and the Americans, the chiefs went home. Franklin then presented a proposal to his twenty-three colonial colleagues—"Short Hints Towards a Scheme for a General Union of the British Colonies on the Continent."

This "General Union" would not get rid of each colony's government. It would add another level of government: a Grand Council of lawmakers from each colony and a President General—much like our Congress and President today.

Franklin cherished the British tradition of elected assemblies that had taken root in American soil. He shared a bit of the prosperity that British culture and trade brought to the colonies. And he believed that "the Foundations of the future Grandeur and Stability of the British Empire, lie in America."

America had vast lands and raw materials. Britain's

industries used those raw materials to produce goods to trade all around the world.

Franklin declared that his General Union of the British Colonies on the Continent, working alongside the British king and Parliament, would transform Great Britain into *Greater* Britain, "the greatest Political Structure Human Wisdom ever yet erected."

For ten days, the twenty-four colonial delegates chewed over Franklin's plan. Questions flew back and forth . . . rich colonies vs. poor colonies . . . large vs. small. What about taxes, defense, trade, the British Parliament? Franklin had answers to all these questions.

After much debate and a few changes, the delegates approved Franklin's plan.

Now came the harder parts. The delegates had to convince their colonial assemblies to approve the General Union. Franklin had to get approval from Parliament in London.

For the next several months, he wrote letters and newspaper articles promoting the General Union. He traveled up and down the colonies trying to convince people that his plan would make the British Empire—including North America—invincible!

But Franklin's idea was too radical in 1754.

A General Union would reduce our power, cried the colonial assemblies. It would be too democratic, sniffed the British.

Every single colony rejected it. So did the British Parliament.

Franklin had failed miserably. But he didn't change his mind. He still believed the British Empire had a great future. And he clung to his idea that "Britain and her Colonies should be considered as one Whole, and not as different

States with separate Interests."

He was still a loyal British subject.

After America fought a revolution and won her independence, a federal government was created alongside the state governments.

In 1789, Franklin wrote: I am still of Opinion it would have been happy for both Sides the Water if [the General Union] had been adopted. . . . the subsequent Pretence for Taxing America, and the bloody Contest it occasioned, would have been avoided. But such Mistakes are not new; History is full of the Errors of States and Princes.

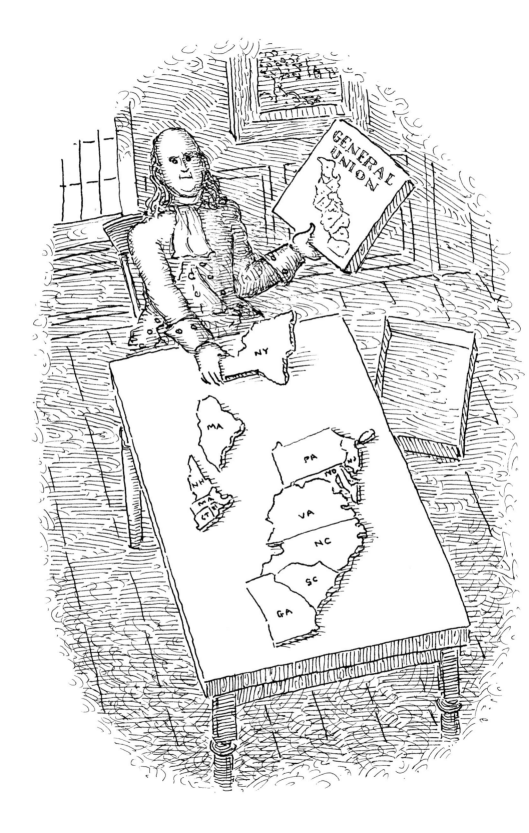

STEP #6

**Benjamin Franklin knew
that uniting the thirteen colonies
would bring fresh strength and power
to both America and Great Britain.**

"The Good-will of the Governed will be starved, if not fed by the good Deeds of the Governors."

Benjamin Franklin found Pennsylvania political life swarming with enemies and feuds. His tactics of cooperation and teamwork didn't always work.

William Penn had founded Pennsylvania in 1681, and his sons still owned huge tracts of land there. But they didn't pay *any* taxes on that land. Farmers and workers like Franklin paid the taxes to fund the government.

Not fair!

The Penns didn't even live in Pennsylvania, but on rich estates in England. Yet they had the power to appoint all officials, create courts, and veto laws.

Really not fair!

The Pennsylvania Assembly—elected by the people—passed laws to tax the Penns' property, but the Penns' hand-picked governors vetoed *every one*.

Absolutely not fair!

So, in 1757, the Assembly sent Franklin to England to talk sense into the Penn family: pay taxes on your land like the rest of the citizens and honor the laws the Assembly passed.

When Franklin arrived in London he found loads of friends there—writers, artists, scientists, merchants—who were thrilled to meet the brilliant American they had heard so much about. He traveled through England, Scotland, and Ireland, and made more friends.

But when he got down to his official business, things got a lot less friendly.

Franklin took his case about the Penns' taxes to the top ranks of the British government. There he got a shock—and not the electrical kind.

"You Americans have wrong Ideas," Lord Granville said. The colonial governors took their orders from British government ministers. Their assemblies had no power to make laws of their own. If Franklin and the Americans thought otherwise, they were mistaken. Britain held complete power over the American colonies. It was as simple as that.

Franklin was flabbergasted!

Next, he met with Thomas and Richard Penn to discuss

taxing their lands. These arrogant, upper-class snobs loathed Franklin on sight. They refused even to consider the issue. Write to our lawyer, Thomas said.

Franklin wrote, describing the Penns' tax situation as "both unjust and cruel." The lawyer ignored him *for a year*.

When Franklin finally got to talk to Thomas Penn again, Franklin declared that the elected members of the Pennsylvania Assembly had "the Rights of the Freeborn Subjects of England" to make laws for Pennsylvania—just as the elected Members of Parliament made laws for England.

Penn sneered at this with "laughing Insolence." Franklin, his blood boiling, didn't dare say a word, but the expression on his face said it all. He looked, the Penns said, "like a malicious V[illain] as he always does." As for Franklin, he felt "a more . . . thorough Contempt for [Penn] than . . . for any Man living."

So far, so bad.

Franklin learned that aristocratic ministers, appointed by the king, ran the government. And they certainly didn't consider Americans equal to British subjects in Great Britain. But Franklin had one more hope—the elected members of the House of Commons in Parliament. They were independent-minded public servants, weren't they? They would be on the side of the Americans, wouldn't they?

No way. The members of parliament did what government ministers told them to do.

Franklin's friends advised him to be patient. That was torture for a man of action like Franklin. "I am oblig'd to wait . . . or take upon myself the Blame of Rashness," he glumly wrote to an American friend.

Months and then years dragged on. Franklin sat through endless hearings and negotiations about nineteen different laws from the Pennsylvania Assembly. In the end five were approved, the rest were thrown out. One of the approved was the right to tax the Penn family, but not too heavily.

Not a complete defeat for Franklin, but hardly a roaring success.

In 1762, after five years, Franklin went home to Philadelphia. But two years later he was back in London, this time working for New Jersey, Georgia, and Massachusetts, as well as Pennsylvania.

And their complaints?

Taxes again! Taxes and more taxes heaped on all the colonies by Parliament.

Opposition spread throughout the colonies—public speeches, petitions to Parliament, newspapers articles, pamphlets, consumer boycotts, peaceful protests, violent riots.

No taxation without representation! the colonists shouted. Only our elected assemblies have the right to tax us. Since we aren't represented in Parliament, you don't have that right!

No taxation without representation? Nonsense, said Parliament. We can do whatever we want, and we want to tax you!

Franklin took up his old weapons, the pen and the press, to defend the colonies. Franklin's serious essays and biting satires flooded London newspapers. But the British government didn't budge.

Then in January of 1774, news arrived of the Boston Tea Party.

More than one hundred men, protesting the British tax on tea, had dumped 342 chests of tea into Boston harbor—worth £10,000 ($2,000,000 today). That gang of rebels lived across the ocean. But the British had a rebel close at hand—Benjamin Franklin.

On January 29, 1774, the Privy Council ordered Franklin to appear before them. The government leaders sat decked

out in powdered wigs and red robes with white fur trim.
Spectators packed the room.

Franklin, wearing a simple blue corduroy suit and his own
gray locks, stood before them.

For more than an hour, a government lawyer threw a
"torrent of virulent abuse" at Franklin.

The audience cheered and jeered.

Franklin said not a word. He refused to dignify their
insults with answers.

His loyalty to Britain was fading fast. He declared,
"While the government is mild and just, while important civil
and religious rights are secure, such subjects will be dutiful
and obedient."

But he warned, "The waves do not rise, but when the
winds blow."

Franklin felt violent winds of oppression blowing from
Britain and saw waves of rebellion rising and crashing over
America. He had spent many years in England trying to calm
those winds, but he had failed.

He sailed home to Pennsylvania in March of 1775 to
warn his countrymen that the ferocious storm from England
showed no signs of dying down. The thirteen colonies must
break free of Great Britain.

STEP #7

**Benjamin Franklin chose revolution
when he saw
that compromise was impossible.**

Revolution!

"Words and Arguments are now of no Use."

By the time Franklin returned home to Philadelphia in 1775, he was a die-hard revolutionary. All thirteen colonies had united to form a Continental Congress—Franklin's old idea. Delegates from every colony met in Philadelphia, but they were still trying to patch up the quarrel with Britain.

Franklin knew better.

He knew that the British had no intention of treating Americans as equals and letting them govern themselves. "Words and Arguments are now of no Use," Franklin said in 1775.

But the Continental Congress dithered for another year, sending King George yet *another* petition that he didn't even

bother to read. John Adams saw Franklin's frustration. Franklin "seems to think us, too irresolute, and backward," Adams said.

Finally, in 1776, the delegates came around to Franklin's view. He helped Thomas Jefferson write the Declaration of

Independence and signed it along with fifty-six other men. They were all traitors now in British eyes.

A famous quote is credited to Franklin: "We must, indeed, all hang together, or, most assuredly, we shall all hang separately."

War!

"Having lived long, I have experienced many instances of being obliged, by better information or fuller consideration, to change opinions even on important subjects, which I once thought right, but found to be otherwise."

General George Washington raised a ragtag Continental Army to fight against the superior British Army and Navy. But Washington kept losing battles. America's only hope was an alliance with Britain's old enemy, France.

So off to Paris sailed seventy-year-old Benjamin Franklin, America's international celebrity. The French loved him on sight. Using his personal charm, canny intellect, clever writings, and unending patience, Franklin convinced King Louis XVI to provide money for arms, equipment, and uniforms for the struggling American army.

Even more important, the French sent soldiers and warships that helped the Americans win the Battle of Yorktown and the surrender of the British Army. Franklin remained in France for nearly ten years, long enough to help write the peace treaty that guaranteed the independence of the United States of America.

On September 3, 1783, British and American officials met to sign that treaty. Benjamin Franklin again stood tall, wearing even grayer locks and the same plain blue corduroy suit he had worn during his public humiliation in London in 1774.

The old revolutionary savored a taste of sweet revenge.

Benjamin Franklin's long road to revolution took many twists and turns:

> running away from Boston,
>
> learning to write brilliant prose,
>
> becoming a community leader,
>
> trying and failing to unite the colonies,
>
> trying and failing to make peace with Britain.

For seventy years, he had cherished that shiny whistle called the British Empire. It had given him chances to grow and prosper more than he ever imagined as a boy. But in the end, Benjamin Franklin, like old Mrs. Silence Dogood, knew that losing his "rights and liberties" was too high a price to pay for any whistle—or any empire.

And he tossed that whistle away.

AUTHOR'S NOTE

Before I began writing for children, I worked as an editorial assistant for *The Papers of Benjamin Franklin,* a vast publishing project at Yale University in Connecticut. Franklin lived for eighty-four years and wrote voluminously for most of those years—essays, satires, almanacs, official documents, and an autobiography. He also wrote and received thousands of letters.

The Franklin Papers, which aims to publish all those writings, began in 1954 and is not scheduled to finish until 2027! For several years, I spent all day with Franklin, copyediting his transcribed letters and fact-checking the footnotes the editors wrote. I spent many evening hours reading more about him. I was smitten.

Wonderful children's books have been written about Benjamin Franklin. There are so many tales to tell about this amazing man. I humbly add mine to the collection, knowing that it won't be the last.

BENJAMIN FRANKLIN'S WORLD

Schooling—At age eight, Franklin entered the Boston Latin School, the best school in town. There he studied English and Latin grammar. He soon rose to the top of his class and skipped to the next grade. Many of his classmates would go on to Harvard College and become church ministers, but Benjamin's father didn't see that path for his  son. Benjamin was too curious, too cheeky. So, a year later, his father sent him to a more practical school to study reading, writing, and arithmetic. At ten years old, after just two years, Benjamin's school days were over. But not his education. His vast learning, including five foreign languages, came from a lifetime of reading and writing. He was one of history's great autodidacts—a self-taught man.

Apprenticeship—Like Franklin, many boys learned a trade, not by going to college, but by learning on the job, usually for seven to nine years. Even doctors and lawyers were trained in offices, not in classrooms. Carpenters, silversmiths, tailors, merchants, and printers like Franklin took on apprentices to work for them. Masters were legally bound to provide clothing, room, and board, and to teach the boys the skills of their trade. They also sent them to school to learn reading, writing, and arithmetic. Girls learned the many skills of housewifery, either from their mothers, or in a stranger's household. Apprentices weren't allowed to visit taverns, gamble, or marry. When they completed their contract, they received clothing, tools, or money.

Frequent newspaper ads for runaway apprentices show that Franklin's escape was not unusual. Apprentices ran away because they felt mistreated, because they thought they knew enough to work for wages, or because they just wanted their freedom. If they were caught, their contract was extended by a year or two. If they left the colony, the master

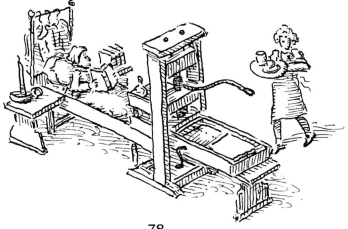

couldn't enforce his contract. James didn't even try to find Benjamin. He knew that his brother would run far enough to gain his freedom.

Printer—For more than thirty years, Franklin donned a leather apron and went to work printing books, newspapers, and pamphlets—and writing them, too. He worked with his hands as well as his head; he used his muscle as well as his brain. Though his later careers—scientist, politician, diplomat—brought him success and fame, he remained proud of his working-class roots. He even set up a small printing press at his home in Paris, France, to print official documents as well as *bagatelles* (short essays) for his friends.

In England and France, Franklin mingled with lords and kings who had never dirtied their hands with manual labor. But, in his last will and testament, he identified himself first not as a world-famous scientist or eminent statesman, but as "Benjamin Franklin of Philadelphia, printer."

Slavery—In the revolutionary era, about 500,000 African Americans—20% of the total population—lived in the American colonies. 450,000 (90%) were enslaved. In the South, plantation owners grew rich from the labor of enslaved men and women. In the North, slave traders and ship owners grew rich transporting Africans to America and the West Indies. These captives were enslaved for life with no legal rights. For a time, Franklin owned a few enslaved household servants. But eventually he renounced slavery and became president of the Pennsylvania Society for Promoting the Abolition of Slavery. Northern states began abolishing slavery after 1780, but it took a bloody Civil War to end it in the South. The Thirteenth Amendment to the US Constitution, passed in 1865, abolished slavery throughout the nation.

Scientific explorations—Franklin's experiments with electricity made him famous, but his boundless curiosity led him in many scientific directions. He made eight trans-Atlantic crossings in his lifetime and used his time to study the sea, sky, and marine life. He kept journals of all his varied observations and shared them with friends in America and Europe. Those journals discussed ship design, ocean currents, wind, storms, dolphins, lunar eclipses, magnetism, comets, circulation of blood, lead poisoning, and more. His inventions reflected his love of the useful—bifocal glasses, a heating stove, an electrical storage battery, and the lightning rod. He even invented a musical instrument— the glass armonica, which used glass discs to create an eerie ringing sound.

How to make a lightning rod—Attach a long iron pointed rod, rising eight feet above the roof, along the outside wall of a building, and sink it four feet into the ground. That, Franklin declared, would guarantee that the building "will not be damaged by Lightning, it being attracted by the Points, and passing thro the Metal into the Ground without hurting any Thing."

Friends in Great Britain—Though he was snubbed by the Penn family and government leaders, Franklin's diverse British friends and admirers included a bishop, several lords, scientists, writers, and philosophers. He found the cultural atmosphere of Britain so stimulating that, for a time, he considered settling there for life. He changed his mind when the British government began undermining the liberties of the American colonies. Franklin grew to despise the ruling politicians of Britain, but he remained faithful to his many British friends.

Pastimes—Franklin's boundless curiosity and love of life led him in many directions in his free time:

Swimming: Young Benjamin was strong and athletic and liked "Running, Leaping, Wrestling, and Swimming, &c." But he loved swimming best. As a teenager, he attracted quite a crowd one day as he swam several miles up and down a river, performing "many Feats of Activity both upon and under Water." Over two centuries later, in 1968, Franklin was elected to the International Swimming Hall of Fame.

Chess: Franklin learned chess as a young man and remained an avid player all his life. During his years in England and France, he often spent his evenings—and even some all-night sessions—playing chess with friends. He wrote an essay called "The Morals of Chess." He considered

the game much more than an "idle amusement." It strengthened many good "qualities of the mind" including foresight (thinking ahead), caution, and persevering in difficult situations. Franklin was eventually elected to the United States Chess Hall of Fame in 1999.

Music: Franklin loved music. He especially liked Scottish folk tunes and made musical arrangements of his favorites. He played duets with his daughter, Sally—she on harpsichord (a keyboard instrument), and he on his invention, the glass armonica. No musical hall of fame includes Franklin, but his glass armonica did inspire Mozart and Beethoven to write music for it. A few composers even write for it today.

TIMELINE
Benjamin Franklin: 1706–1790

1706—January 17, born in Boston, youngest son of Josiah and Abiah Franklin.

1718—Finishes his two years of schooling. Signs on as an apprentice to his brother James Franklin, a printer, for nine years.

1723—Runs away from Boston to Philadelphia; works for printer Samuel Keimer.

1724—Travels to London to buy printing equipment, but money promised to him doesn't arrive. Works as a printer.

1726—Returns to Philadelphia and Keimer's print shop.

1727—Forms the Junto, a self-improvement society for young tradesmen.

1728—Establishes his own printing business.

1729—Begins publishing *The Pennsylvania Gazette.*

1730—Appointed official printer for Pennsylvania. Marries Deborah Read.

1731—Establishes the Library Company. Birth of son William.

1732—Birth of son Francis (Franky).

1732–58—*Poor Richard's Almanack* published.

1735—Brother James dies. Franklin sends his widow 500 free copies of *Poor*

Richard to sell. Brings nephew Jemmy to Philadelphia to become his apprentice.

1736—Son Francis dies of smallpox.

1737—Appointed Postmaster of Philadelphia.

1740—Appointed official printer of New Jersey.

1743—Birth of daughter Sarah (Sally).

1748—Retires from printing business to concentrate on electricity experiments.

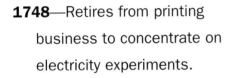

1751—Report of his electrical research published in London. Elected to Pennsylvania Assembly.

1752—Conducts kite/lightning experiment.

1753—Receives honorary college degrees from Harvard and Yale and the Copley Medal from the Royal Society of London.

1754—Proposes "Scheme for a General Union of the British Colonies" that is rejected by colonial assemblies and Parliament.

1757—Travels to England as agent for Pennsylvania.

1759—Receives honorary degree of Doctor of Laws from University of St. Andrews, Scotland.

1762—Receives honorary degree of Doctor of Civil Laws from University of Oxford, England. Returns to Pennsylvania.

1764—Returns to England as colonial agent for Pennsylvania, New Jersey, Georgia, and Massachusetts.

1771—Begins writing his *Autobiography*.

1774—Deborah Read, his wife of 44 years, dies.

1775—Returns to Philadelphia. Elected to Continental Congress. War breaks out in Massachusetts. George Washington forms Continental Army.

1776—Works with Thomas Jefferson to write Declaration of Independence. Independence declared. Travels to Paris, France as Commissioner of Congress.

1778—Signs an alliance between the United States and France.

1783—Signs peace treaty with England.

1785—Returns to Philadelphia.

1787—Joins Constitutional Convention, signs US Constitution. Becomes president of Pennsylvania Society for Promoting the Abolition of Slavery.

1790—In February, presents abolition petition to Congress. On April 17, dies in Philadelphia.

RESEARCH BIBLIOGRAPHY

*All quotations used in the book can be found in the following sources marked with an asterisk (*).

*Bowen, Catherine Drinker. *The Most Dangerous Man in America: Scenes from the Life of Benjamin Franklin*. Boston: Little, Brown, 1974.

*Boyd, Julian P., ed. *Indian Treaties Printed by Benjamin Franklin, 1736–1762*. Philadelphia: Historical Society of Pennsylvania, 1938.

Bunker, Nick. *Young Benjamin Franklin: The Birth of Ingenuity*. New York: Knopf, 2018.

Cohen, I. Bernard. *Benjamin Franklin's Science*. Cambridge: Harvard University Press, 1990.

*Franklin, Benjamin. *The Autobiography of Benjamin Franklin*. New Haven: Yale University Press, 1964.

*Franklin, Benjamin. *The Bagatelles from Passy*. New York: Eakins Press, 1967.

*Franklin, Benjamin. *Poor Richard's Almanack*. New York: Skyhorse Publishing, 2007.

Goodwin, George. *Benjamin Franklin in London: The British Life of America's Founding Father*. London, Weidenfeld & Nicolson: 2017.

Greene, Jack P. "Pride, Prejudice, and Jealousy: Benjamin Franklin's Explanation for the American Revolution," in *Reappraising Benjamin Franklin: A Bicentennial Perspective*. Edited by J. A. Lemay. Newark: University of Delaware Press, 1993, 119–142.

*Isaacson, Walter. *Benjamin Franklin: An American Life*. New York: Simon & Schuster, 2003.

Lepore, Jill. *The Story of America*. Princeton: Princeton University Press, 2012.

Lerner, Ralph. *The Thinking Revolutionary: Principle and Practice in the New Republic*. Ithaca: Cornell University Press, 1988.

Morgan, Edmund S. *Benjamin Franklin*. New Haven, Yale University Press: 2002.

The Papers of Benjamin Franklin. The American Philosophical Society and Yale University. franklinpapers.org.

BIBLIOGRAPHY FOR
YOUNG READERS

Barretta, Gene. *Now & Ben: The Modern Inventions of Benjamin Franklin*. New York: Henry Holt, 2006.

Byrd, Robert. *Electric Ben: The Amazing Life and Times of Benjamin Franklin*. New York: Dial, 2012.

Fisher, Leonard Everett. *The Printers: A Short History*. New York: Benchmark/Cavendish, 2000.

Fleming, Candace. *Ben Franklin's Almanac: Being a True Account of the Good Gentleman's Life*. New York: Atheneum, 2003.

Freedman, Russell. *Becoming Ben Franklin: How a Candle-Maker's Son Helped Light the Flame of Liberty*. New York: Holiday House, 2013.

Rockliff, Mara. *Mesmerized: How Ben Franklin Solved a Mystery that Baffled All of France*. Somerville, MA: Candlewick, 2015

Rosenstock, Barb. *Ben Franklin's Big Splash: The Mostly True Story of His First Invention*. Honesdale PA: Calkins Creek, 2014.

Schroeder, Alan. *Ben Franklin: His Wit and Wisdom from A–Z*. New York: Holiday House, 2011.

WEBSITES*

Websites active at time of publication

benjaminfranklinhouse.org.

> Franklin's London residence is now a small museum.

Grundhauser, Eric. "Keeping the Ethereal Sounds of the Glass Armonica Alive." atlasobscura.com/articles/ben-franklin-singing-bowl-glass-armonica.

> Videos of present-day glass armonica performers.

nps.gov/inde/planyourvisit/benjaminfranklinmuseum.htm.

> Museum on the site of Franklin's home in Philadelphia.

nps.gov/inde/planyourvisit/printingoffice.htm.

> A working 18th-century-style printing office at the Franklin Museum.

pbs.org/benfranklin/index.html.

> A comprehensive site filled with information about many facets of Franklin's life.

printmuseum.org.

> Executive Director Mark Barbour and staff have recreated an 18th-century printshop that Franklin would recognize. Demonstrations using historical printing equipment are presented in person and on YouTube. "Benjamin Franklin" (aka Phil Soinski) gives engaging talks to visitors. A traveling Museum on Wheels also takes the show on the road to schools.

Rose, P. K. "The Founding Fathers of American Intelligence." cia.gov/static/4c28451b90165b446ac948e3dd47c972/The-Founding-Fathers-of-American-Intelligence-.pdf.

> A CIA report on Franklin's covert actions in France during the American Revolution.

Scallon, Rob. "Glass Armonica (spinning glass bowls... that break)." youtube.com/watch?v=cVqqNiglmtU.

> Detailed video showing how musician Dennis James made a glass armonica and how to play it.

ACKNOWLEDGMENTS

Of the thousands of books written about Benjamin Franklin, none is more engaging than his *Autobiography*. But, after more than two centuries, authors are still finding new things to say about our most charming, eclectic, and cosmopolitan Founding Father. Nick Bunker's book, *Young Benjamin Franklin: The Birth of Ingenuity*, has been especially valuable to me in my research. Nick has also been kind enough to read my manuscript and save me from what Franklin called "errata."

My venerable writers' group—going strong since 1992—once again offered critiques of many drafts of this book. Caroline Arnold, Sherrill Kushner, Alexis O'Neill, and Ann Stampler have become both esteemed colleagues and dear friends. Carolyn Yoder, best of editors, has steered another of my books into print with insight and enthusiasm. Thanks also to the Calkins Creek team for their part in bringing this book to life. And I'm thrilled to have John O'Brien, master illustrator and proud Philadelphian, join me in celebrating my old flame, Benjamin Franklin.

ILLUSTRATOR'S NOTE

I was born in Philadelphia (the city of Benjamin Franklin!) and was constantly aware of his history there—his inventions, the institutions he started, the places he lived and worked, and the ideas he came up with. His presence is everywhere in the city. As an illustrator and cartoonist, this rich history offers me a treasure trove of material to inspire ideas for my drawings. Fortunately, I still live near Philadelphia, which proved very helpful in bringing this incredible and ingenious American revolutionary to life—step by step!

GRETCHEN WOELFLE is an award-winning author of fiction and nonfiction books for young readers. She is most awfully curious—some would say nosy—about people who do extraordinary things. Some, like Benjamin Franklin, are already famous. Others should be more famous. Her biographies include *A Take-Charge Girl Blazes a Trail to Congress: The Story of Jeannette Rankin*; *Answering the Cry for Freedom: Stories of African Americans and the American Revolution*; and *Mumbet's Declaration of Independence*. When she is not traveling the world looking for new stories, Gretchen lives in Los Angeles, California. Visit gretchenwoelfle.com.

JOHN O'BRIEN has illustrated more than 100 books for children including *Revolutionary Rogues* by Selene Castrovilla, *Thomas Jefferson Builds a Library* by Barb Rosenstock, and *Look . . . Look Again!* by himself. He has also contributed cartoons to *The New Yorker* since 1987. John lives in Delran, New Jersey. Visit johnobrienillustrator.com.

For information about permission to reproduce selections form this book, please
contact permissions@astrapublishinghouse.com.

Publisher's Cataloging-in-Publication data

Names: Woelfle, Gretchen, author. | O'Brien, John, 1953-, illustrator.
Title: How Benjamin Franklin became a revolutionary in seven (not-so-easy) steps /
written by Gretchen Woelfle; illustrated by John O'Brien.
Description: Includes bibliographical references. | New York, NY: Calkins Creek, an
imprint of Astra Books for Young Readers, 2023.
Identifiers: LCCN: 2022949700 | ISBN: 9781635923315 (hardcover) |
9781635925524 (ebook)
Subjects: LCSH Franklin, Benjamin, 1706-1790–Juvenile literature. | United
States–History–Revolution, 1775-1783–Juvenile literature. | United States–Politics
and government–1775-1783–Juvenile literature. | Statesmen–United States–Biogra-
phy–Juvenile literature. | BISAC JUVENILE NONFICTION / Biography & Autobiography
/ Historical | JUVENILE NONFICTION / Biography & Autobiography / Political |
JUVENILE NONFICTION / History / United States / Colonial & Revolutionary Periods
Classification: LCC E302.6.F8 .W64 2023 | DDC 973.3/092–dc23

Calkins Creek
An imprint of Astra Books for Young Readers, a division of Astra Publishing House
astrapublishinghouse.com
Printed in China

ISBN: 978-1-63592-331-5 (hc)
ISBN: 978-1-63592-552-4 (eBook)
Library of Congress Control Number: 2022949700

First edition

10 9 8 7 6 5 4 3 2 1

Design by Barbara Grzeslo
The text is set in Franklin Gothic.
The titles are set in Bodoni Bold.
The illustrations are done with Rapidograph pens and ink on Strathmore 500 series
vellum Bristol Board. The cover illustrations are done similarly but with Doctor
Martin's Hydrus Watercolors added.